MW00910044

Ken Belford

Decompositions

Talonbooks

Talonbooks
Box 2076, Vancouver, British Columbia, Canada V6B 3S3
www.talonbooks.com

Typeset in Veljović and printed and bound in Canada.
Printed on 100% post-consumer recycled paper.

First Printing: 2010

The publisher gratefully acknowledges the financial support of the Canada Council for
the Arts; the Government of Canada through the Book Publishing Industry Development
Program; and the Province of British Columbia through the British Columbia Arts Council
and the Book Publishing Tax Credit for our publishing activities.

Library and Archives Canada Cataloguing in Publication

Belford, Ken, 1946–
 Decompositions / Ken Belford.

Poems.
ISBN 978-0-88922-631-9

 I. Title.

PS8503.E47D43 2010   C811'.54   C2009-906977-6

for Si

Earlier versions of some of these sequences have appeared in the Association for Literature and Study of the Environment net journal, The Goose, *and in Capilano University Editions'* Open Text: Canadian Poetry and Poetics in the 21st Century, *volume 2, ed. Roger Farr. Additionally, two pieces appeared in Jay MillAr's* BafterC, *and one other in Kemeny Babineau's journal,* The New Chief Tongue.

Thanks go to the BC Arts Council for a writing grant which greatly assisted me in the time and work it took to bring these pages together. Thanks also to the Canada Council for a writing grant which sustains my endeavours.

It just happens the idea
of meaning exists only
in fiction, where it takes on
a life of its own. The evolution
of the living image pleases
our dispositions but the pliable
appearance does not walk around
on the ground and lives only in
the fictional world of flashback
and dream. The reality is, scenes
take place, and these impossible
events, these replications of
objects that are not very much
like the world are secondhand
experiences, an idea, a likeness
of scenery, or an event staged
in front of a microphone.

I was a man, the story goes, who needed
a name, but before I get to it, let me tell you
the stories about my other name.
My pen name was Ken.
Some of you follow my name around.
My poems are my only property.
I was unsuccessful at love and work,
but was generous with my money
and gave it away as it came in.
Stories were written about me,
but narratives were imposed on my work
and all of them ignored my complexity.
I pissed out the windows of my friends,
puked on the doorstep of my neighbour,
and drank in the local dive.
My name was an empty space
but according to one version,
Si followed me home to Hazelton
and went up to me as I reached my tent.
When my poems are read out
it is in the context of my name story.
I have had to cope with competing narratives
but my name was chosen by me
and the variations of the tale
are my attempts to explain him.

If even one thing had been different
we might have known of outcome bias
and corrected our paths before the consequences
and tradeoffs. If we had known
of the nature of error and small failures.
If we could look back and remember
when systems fail we live the same pattern over,
and know bungles are understandable, that
misprints are not random events, but near misses,
and know whoever is closest to the error is not
the reason for the failure.
Knowledge can remain inert when needed,
and stay switched off.
Blunders occur in combinations.
It's not always the assistant
who's the source of the error,
but when I broke free of assumptions,
I realized an error is a starting point,
and love, resembling wonder, is
the trajectory of buggy accidents.
Oh, incidents evolve, and
signs come in over many noisy feeds.

Most of the risks I take are voluntary
but I remember disasters I lived through
that still can't be understood.
I didn't live at the wrong time
or in the wrong place,
like along the Skeena flood line,
or even in a dangerous place,
but I saw the wildfires of the Nass
and lived in a handmade home on a steep slope
that looked like the upper Volta.
Income continues when
the canyons of the rich slough away in flood.
It takes money to buy design
but risk is the common thread.
I lived in a flimsy economy
and made my home where settlement had been.
Everything varies from disturbance to disturbance,
but the gap I mean is widening.
Systems of class are more dangerous than natural disasters,
but our families were failures
and we needed to get away from them,
so we took refuge in the mountains.

Pathogens jump when ecosystems change
but the population is naïve
when it enters an area of infection.
Compared with others,
the type of contact I lived was not
a food, or family, or animal contact route,
but evolved from a common ancestor.
Today I write poems that have high mutation rates.
I'm a new type that became more common,
an old sequence recopied upstream
in a new strand that follows flooding
and I'm good at attaching to surfaces.
There isn't much mutation
in the housekeeping genes.
I'm integrating in through recombinations
as a naked piece of DNA in the environment,
not passed vertically
from generation to generation,
but by means of the conjugation of plasmids
into the occupation of the new.

There is reason to share this
world with others. Animals are
not so different after all. For much
of my life I lived in wild places
that had nothing to do with anyone.
I wasn't ready to be viewed, refused
to adapt, and made common cause
with the animals at the outlet, where
I transgressed the imagined and
resisted the ordered metaphors
of threat. To glimpse something
of these places that run between
phenomena is to interrupt the flow
of the narrative. It's animals that
have a sense of place and I'm a
river rhino, an insurgent kept against
my will. I own many books of stuffed
parts. All my life I lost the point,
and I resist when I take my time
and amble in and out of rules.

An accidental invader,
low to the ground and covered with dew,
she came across a grassy field,
then through my window
and into my bedroom
first thing in the morning
but I was bit at night
when the sky was overcast.
One wound and I wept,
then skipped about
before slipping into
an undisciplined dance.
She lived in the town
at the tip of the island.
Her stout, long legs,
her literary jaw,
her dark brown body,
her broad flat hair,
her green eyes shone.

Without a known destination,
I could not speak, or think,
or write in a coherent way,
but now, still not understood,
but passed on by suggestion,
I'm somehow more explicable.
The world owes me a living.
Only sickness gets time off work.
Work's not my job.
I'd rather anything but work.
Illnesses need to be romantic,
and tap in to fashions.
The problem is, capitalism
is a transient virus, a disease
requiring complicity of community,
but if it is to work and
not be an epidemic,
a quarantine is needed.

Market forces dictate what it costs to
flip a switch. It's called the exchange rate
in the news, but market forces dictate
the level of penetration. Trends go up
faster than they come down unless
the sustainable level of the price of gas falls
below the national baselines of poverty
and ecosystem degradation. Management
poetry works the social hours, taking up
space and attention in classrooms and
academic journals, but the shanty dwellers
are unregulated and not influential.
Market forces dictate what you do, but first
you have to know enough to get started.

Only the few who have adjusted the models
even know what nonmarket poetry is.
Market forces dictate product demands
and the organization of supply chains,
the crops grown, the final product, and
the policy rules. Regulations are about
the price of land, what happens, where
the passenger gateways are, outcomes
like health fees and the price of
washing machines. Market forces dictate
standards in industry, the dominant use
of the land, and where freight goes.
The United States is content to let
market forces dictate coal will continue
to be used for electricity. Market forces
dictate the type of people who will purchase
new homes, and ensures that business people
who meet their financial requirements
receive preference. Transportation networks,
geography, and market forces dictate
the pressure to commit to more work hours,
but market forces dictate name changes,
immigration policy, and pay.

Capital is the tender and run of rules
but it isn't worth it, and the refusal of
form is the side effect of the narrative
handed over every day, forced
beyond the dissymmetry between
my concrete self and remembering
I used to be a vegan but I met a girl
who used to be a vegan. I gave her a gift,
a copy of my book. I said I'm working,
just not working for you. To expect
gifts from those I have not given to is
not unlike trying to turn poetry into
cash by turning it into reality but
something else that matters more is
how the object of sentiment turns into
commodities, and how I never broke
down and craved a hot meatball sub.
I used to be vegan but I got married
and caved after I ran over a duck but
I haven't killed through default since.

As far back as I know, convictions
are not got, but earned, and unlike
what I remember, should not be
confused with new memories of love
or the wetlands on the little farm
I was born to, where intrusive images
of experience, ambush, and combat
get glued together by narrative.
Places come and places go and I
don't know if narrative is pretty
good at what happened but I live
in a culture that is a grand abstraction
of illness narratives and exploits
facing scenery. It's not the whole story,
but iron loses its power when the past
intrudes into the present. Today
I took out a map and visited my
old place without leaving home.
I've always been an outsider with
a map in my hands. Now I live in
a region in front of mountains.
I wonder about those who replicate
the landscapes of exclusion, who
write the geographies of power,
the poems of detachment and expanse,
background writings of scenery and
setting, about as much as can be seen.

To be a Harlequin is to be
in a local form,
Harlequin, I knew you'd go,
I knew you'd fade,
but who could know
I'd want to be invisible like you,
to not hold back
and travel anywhere,
and take on other forms.
But light areas fill with wolf whistle
and blue merle, blue merle
there are many shades of blue.
Daughters are a modifier and
there are no photos of the others,
but when I saw my Harlequin,
I was thinking of you,
remembering shades of grey
in much the same way
as the Harley I glimpsed
before it flew.

Primarily about the distribution of light,
realism is a synthetic noise called grey
that makes use of an orthodox theology,
images forced to lie on slabs of light.
Realistic images are filtered through grey
levels before light leaves the apparent
object on the way to bias. It's one of the
synthetic examples of fashion hardware,
but belief (reaching out without selling out)
is the reason for poetry. When the viewpoint
is fixed, even the depth estimates are
conservative. And if the resolution of the
output image is the same as the input image,
then the illumination of the generated image
is grey, grey (Wong, Browne et al., 2008).

What took place was the second-storey wall
collapsed onto the first,
and then onto cars.
A tank farm burned and
the displacements weakened deposits
that spread laterally away
from the centre to the edge.
In every sense of the word,
sections of the interchange
started out for the apparent.
The thoughts that crossed my mind
as I salvaged items from the rubble
were of the sentence,
the habitual custom of debt,
and the stern reappearance
of the likeness—
measures of a deceptive,
out-of-order slash and crash text
after the muscle of order broke down.

The paperwork seemed in order
but I wasn't working,
still one of the many,
a resampled image
revised downward.
At first I thought
I might have fallen
into the spectral orders,
or worse,
a nearly continuous array of prizes
announced in reverse.
But then I wandered out
to where the monotonic
pathologies of images aren't necessary.
I'm still a continual and noisy fit
to the raw, even though
a major portion of the image is missing.

It is this. There are barriers
within all things,
densities in streams
having to do with
the relationship between abundance
and habitat,
and this homogenous variance becomes,
like me, the surrogate measure.
I'm the simpler second model,
not the sum of the men
or the mean, not the egg-to-fry.
But here and there
the lower valley slopes, and
the uncertainties in the upper Nass means
abundancy is typical in the lower reaches
where the water is deep.
When summer is late and
the channel narrows,
and the pools of the streams in the area
dry up, always
they may or may not be.

Many watersheds are not closed,
but when the forests are cut and
burned for conversion to pastures,
the toxic flow paths leach the sand
and clay of my valley and I think of
the timing of losses and the cattle
of secondary growth. The weathered
old soils where I lived were cycled
below the forest cover like I was.
Land use changes—I'm a sixty-five-
year-old forest and my watersheds
pulse. I'm plant available, an example
that isn't representative, not so abundant,
and preferentially lost in a nonconservative
cycle. I know about losses through fire
and forest to pasture conversion, and
these large mats of grass called clearings,
but I do not actively cycle within
the system where I live on tough
lowland soils, which are not flat.

Before I understood the overstory
structure, I lived among the poor
that result from deforestation, on
the edge of an abandoned pasture
seeded with aggressive grasses.
Many transitional families live
awhile by the forest edge wherever
there are remnant trees on the un-
productive land around the city.
Out on the patches I mean, pastures
are prone to burn, ridge and valley
are controlled by fern, and
drying leads to abandonment,
increasing fragmentation. Several
authors could have an impact on
the abrupt decline of diversity, but
luckily trees fall in storms and
fire burns them later. In the valley,
introduced grasses are a barrier
to succession. The seeds that fall
into abandoned areas are not
enough, and it is only much later
when trees slowly shade grasses out,
the large disturbance of cattle is
replaced by the regenerating trees.

I am a big tree with small seeds and
my birds sing the age of an old field.
There is a balance between dispersal,
and relevance, and poetry. I write about
gap dynamics, and I live on the border
of abundance of any abandoned pasture
up to a hundred years old. I speak the
continuous explanatory of the variable
and have no liking for cattle. I live
the differences between distances from
the forest to the field where R is for
recovery and S is for saplings and shrubs.
The longer the abandonment, the greater
the similarity of form. Trees die and leave
gaps. Gaps were frequent where I lived.
The fields outside these cities are adjacent
to forest fragments. I write about the rate
of colonization between distances and
the small gaps of my mornings when
the unrelated cycles back to the border.

C is for the corner where
conditional lines converge,
and the chain made of links
and rods, except in Tennessee.
The bush men of Tennessee
wear pantyhose and have no
authority over unoccupied lands.
An indigenous hybrid, I'm derived
from the animals who run away
when they see you. I will say
what I think. A wolf decided to
walk with me. They keep lists.
C is for company. You go up and
north at the same time. Everything
that lives acts in a particular way
and has a reason to live.

There are mountains, hills,
complexities and plateaus,
but the turning point I mean
was when I was no longer
restricted by landforms, when
I understood the uncertainty
of calculations and the soil and
water loss out on the plateau.
In different morphopoetic regions,
entropy can be given as follows—
the watershed divides, determining
borders, and I write topology indices
of elongated lowland lines, including
mean gullies, but I do not gather
skeletons because the land is not empty.

The aggressive impulses of
the lyric load the details
of the story with what seems
to be a post-dating hangover,
and my shifting trust of order's
single-file chain of incidents
and sequences of ancestors
I'm not about, or lost in thought
with, even if humming in a
line, is about the distinction
apart from which comfort
finds form, and not successions
of fatuous sentiment, but how
I found tools in an empty street,
found money by accident,
watched anger, found company,
cracked open systematic episodes,
and deviated from the expected.

Looks kill and species go extinct
but I look at you and you look at me,
and looks can kill your career,
so don't go to Kenya now.
A holiday isn't worth dying for.
Images shape spectacle and
looking is a turbulent thing.
One leaves off where the other begins.
It's called deregulation
but it depends on who you read.
My hair gets caught in the trees
and I can't hold up my head.
I'm waiting for the moment
when the gang boss goes.
I won't be following the sightseer
on a round trip,
or the eco-tourist who wants to see it all.
Everyone's wanting to go somewhere
but I'll be staying home.

It's as if matter empties to a likeness
when the moving parts of the story
intersect. When I think of you, I see you
the way you were, as someone I knew,
as suggestion in motion, no remainder
left over. When the telegrapher's key
isn't in contact, and pauses in the space
that lies between words, the space that
holds the promise to make sense contains
inaccuracies, as I do. I can't contain
myself when the emotions in the image
move from compassion to sadness and
plot is still in passage and time is
tempo's reform. The representative line
is a grim cabaret, and I am inattentive.

To argue that rural people are ambiguous
does not abandon all as masquerades
about who gets what, but titles change
when the labour debts are called, features
are recognized, place is imagined, and
meaning is made out of landmarks
on the factory floor. It's true there's
too much theory and not enough passion.
Governments take revenue from the poor
even when the granaries are empty.
Culture is in a hurry, and who can ignore
the expectations that go with gifts and
loans, the casual pathways and shallow
groupings? And the types who police
the boundaries of those repressive
cultural forms, who think to regulate
the production and distribution of poetry,
I wish would have to go elsewhere
and beg for work like I did. But now
my assets are intangible, my granaries
hidden, and I mean to throw doubt
on their households and claims.

The deprived can't afford
workshops, particularly when
the price of sentiment is
the virtuous fiction of retreat.
The expressive vectors of
persuasion help make the
pathetic poems of the bourgeoisie,
but landscape is the pet of
nature poetry, and publishing is
the abduction of animals, so
I can't help but like it when
someone steals a dog for ransom,
and I think it's funny when
propertied outrage spills over
into the streets, even if
the form of pets has to do
with the price of love when
they are off the leash and
shitting on the sidewalk.

I'm no expert but I know about animals,
about the line that separates the pen
from the open, about how they are imagined,
how animals are located in the kitchen
or the cage, and how zoos supply animals
to homes. Bears and wolves have walked
with me. Wolves and lions are not the
approved residents of the rolling pasture
lands. Poems in which animals appear
as food are the cows of occupied fields.
There are no dangerous animals in
the jungles of the Nass, and they are
not numerous, except in the dreams
of migrants. I'm not as close as my lover
is to the cats and dogs of the city but
a field is a cage and pets cross the street.

When I was poor and lived in the mountains,
I ate the animals who lived there, but
in the city some animals are friends and
some are food. No more than a few of
the people I know have hunted, and
most have pets. They get their meat
in the killed and ready-to-eat form.
Often I test the limits of the household.
Often I think of familial captivity.
There is wilderness in the urban
landscape. Downtown Prince George
at night, for example. In Smithers
I was avoided, and my place was off
the map. I belonged out of sight.
The geospheres of longing and trade
are unable to get along and I am
sympathetic to trans-species, overgrown
gardens, and fragmentation and loss, and
of the conflicts and pathways toward coexistence.

I carried a swan and a leg of a bear on
my back. I had a beard, and cut my hand.
My hair fell to my shoulders. Bony, with
indigo eyes, I spoke no French, and
ventured into town, after a kiss, followed
by a fever. Hunters are the interface there,
and their families, who eat bushmeat,
are suspicious of outsiders. But when
hunters carry home the dead for dinner,
the contact of blood spreads to the next.
Hunters want to get their hands in the blood.
Eventually someone will collect bloodlines
from the hunters and their kills, but it will be
too late. When a virus tries, and fails,
the unborn live on in the mud at the end
of the lake. Not unlike poets, most of
the undiscovered are harmless, but some
are dangerous, or some are known, some not.
The blood on the backs of the men spreads
through family into words, where they elude
surveillance until packaged and shipped.

These are the fevers that go with harm,
that are on or in the mutants
that live in the hosts, that go
with the vectors that sail from cat to cat
and to horse, to pig to bird, and human
they go. From farm to farm the stillborn
go, the down with a bug at the mouth
of the river by way of the cycles
in the blood of bats and crows.
These are the sickly, the infected,
the germy and ill and this is about
the surges of infection that spread
in the lungs and brains and hearts
that go from hand to mouth, that
jump the fence. They jump from a rat
or a bat or a horse, and the sequences
replicate from pest to pest, from
sheep and goats with pox and measles
and rodents and flies. By military contact
they go. And we swap infections
with money. Wherever the colonizer
on horseback goes, death follows, and
the time and the scale is global now that
we reproduce more and parent less.

Robert Johnson let loose the pigs
of Crawford County. They didn't
walk to Wisconsin on their own.
Pigs are not particular and
I don't know what an elk farm is,
but the wild pigs of Wisconsin
should be shot on sight like
the armadillos of Tennessee.
Vaccines and drugs won't help
when a new threat spills over.
Pigs and bats and logging roads
are agents of influenza in the
houses of the poor, and more
and more dirty hunters are
looking for something to kill
at the end of the logging roads.
Microbes pool in the farms
on the edge of the bush.
There's too much logging
and too many farms, and now
when the frequency of contact
steps up, it's good roads bring
health care in because the
villages are going to need it.

When the signs of trouble appear,
everything that happened is forgotten.
Farming is uncertain. Swine flu is
a disease of poverty, the lagoons
have a habit of leaking, and
the pig is an expert in risk.
Mutant fears, mixed with human
strains, sequence from worry
to panic. One is the deception
of production, two is the coincidence
of millions, three is the organisms
in the bodies of the pigs. Farmers
shouldn't buy livestock blind,
but they are blinded by likeness
and the light. Pigs are the slaves
in the barn and tomorrow's the day
ambulances won't pick up the sick.

One and one makes something new
for the lovesick who flee the light
and choose to live alone and write
the misery that originates in love,
picking bones with a loved other
until one dies or the other quits.
Until then her suffering becomes his,
her sensations, his skin, her loss
his eyes, her sweat, his body, her
death, his agony. Once I knew
her name, but the pointing of a stick
could not make me die, or a cabal
of conviction and sentiment, or
love's dark virus in a milder form.

How can a pointed stick do harm,
how, between the subject and the object,
how can the sameness that exists
between hostile shakes and bones
be not complicit, how the meaningless
muttering, the twisted hands and
rolling eyes not be the pestis and
poison of the lyric? I keep a knife and
piece of wood for travelling abandoned
places, and when two and two make
something new, it's of something not
from whittling. I'd rather change my name
and live outside, and wander land in
boredom than suffer in a monastery.

It's best to blink and learn to forget
if it's arcadia or aecidia, best to be
happy, and forget the topological terms
of day, the derivatives of night, and
let the pre-existing ideal slip your mind
and be bygone, and accommodate
the misfit. Images are nomadic.
and you resemble someone I knew.
Keep this not in memory because
volunteer memory is unpaid help
and it fragments. Collective memories
are what makes happiness tick, but
when I write, I forget the poems I like.
Only those who are loyal are allowed
to live on the land and write poems
about it, and those who are not must
leave. Look across the wide, digressive
sward, but don't write about special
places, you'll just make it worse. Best
re-order what the US takes for granted
and take a pay cut to make it happen.

I'm the woman who writes
on the back of photos
nobody wanted to keep.
Each tells a little story
nobody knows anything about.
I like to be invisible
and travel anywhere
and take on other forms.
You can see me with another man
in '56 in front of famous places.
Expectations about
what we are supposed to see
is story litter, flyers.
Look at me.
I travelled a lot.
I wonder about generations.

I wasn't invited to speak
after they heard I was on
plasma, but I was young
and getting to know the
workers behind the wall.
Nature is a lifestyle Photo-
shop retouches, but in the
spaces I infiltrated, in the
grit of the ambient medium,
no one could foresee the
inevitability of starvation,
even though the imaginary
environment is a neglected
area, in itself a puzzling
contradiction, and the raw
material for buildings out
on the server farms. But
resistance burns and love
floods when the mood swings
and the delivery pathways,
fraternal messages jumbled
into rules, give way to first
person and run away for
simplicity outside my door.

But I'm exhausted from
reading books whose pages
trace the progressively fatal
disease of serious writing,
especially the busy poem in
which every moment counts.
How short the surface of the
page when words are only
one-dimensional. In the under-
appreciated books I like,
meaning is measured by
saying no to the demands
of the possessive poem. Who
says good writing conveys
a strong sense of place?
The apparent attempts at
moral instruction from poets
who do not own their own
lives makes me think that about
is *control*, which is why I'm
not convenient, and more
temporary, why I long to be
idle and purposely dormant,
and accelerate away from
those empty places country
does not allow escape from.

People decay, and my memories of you
are mostly clutter. I'm not sure, but
I think I might have left my memories
of you sitting on a window sill.
Something happened, cues moved.
I was out of step when I entered
into marriage. The sore toe on my
dancing partner's foot became
cellular debris. Since then, my
withered marriage cells are incidental
findings, like something that shouldn't
be there. It's like another hand
picked a random note from the clutter.
The old often interferes with the new
but I'm not wanting to borrow a turn
and be remembered one more time.
You didn't stick to anything but yourself,
and you creep toward a puddle left
behind, like a thinking putty in my fridge.

To have brought moving displays into
the account creates perceptual dispositions
of a simple materialism not of the natural
world, but meaning, being mostly affinities,
picks up fast and runs with the grain. It's
a hard-line narrative scheme we pay to watch
and hold ourselves apart from, and I'm thankful
it hasn't yet sentenced us to death with a
pretty picture along the lines of nature poetry.
The poems I like are not visually engaging
the first time heard but we know there is
much sorting of shapes and versions to come
before the end of the story, so we're waiting
for appealing curves, knowing curves meet
and fail. What gripper gloves are to hands,
the moving image is to mind. Discernment
is subject to influence when the still moves
and the moving image morphs into text. The
institutional discourse about what a work
of art means is interrupted. In time, what was
once incomprehensible becomes known, but
for now this film of family misleads and gives
us the slip, this manipulation of images and
events hatched over a small piece of ground.

The simplest explanation is, the islands
lying off the west coast go only in one
direction—toward the point at which
form vanishes. Cinema, cinema, this
film of what we fear becoming is of
the leads who make the poems. Tension
becomes infinite when nothing new
happens. Landscape is an idyllic place
in the imagination, a claim of meaning
farmed by old fogeys. I'm looking, not
for a theory that allows for duplication,
but a consonance that's better. There's
a symmetry beyond the plains and
valleys. Everything that is, is a curiosity
that cascades. I'm forever in potential,
always wandering around, getting to
the top, and rolling down the other side.

In the story you and I are the relevant features
shown together in the image, a simultaneous
display seen and seen through at the same time.
There's always another story, another collection
of things for others to see, another correspondence
using the opaque texture of carefully chosen lines,
and what follows. By making lines explicit,
writers put in what people think they see, but
the local rapid rate of change, and the variable
torque of comprehension curves, and isn't anything
like a line drawing because the shading is a depth
cue using local measures that turn attention
away from line of sight, away from the transparent
surfaces of display, to everything at once.

Most of my neighbours are refugees and
live a differential between the roadside
and the cities of the coast. Here is nowhere
now, a complex of dislocations, the price
of animals falls, and the help quits. I met
writers who, without asking, intercepted
people with stories they said took place,
publishing depictions of symbolic countryside
with staged attractions. Most take the safer
route, claiming friendship, telling phony
travel tales about the people they love.
Destination books influence the language
of the subject, but sexuality limits the poor.
Some live on land of low potential. Others
before have cut the trees and sold the fish.
My neighbours are equally poor, but not
equally vulnerable. Sometimes the people
can't feed themselves. Food hasn't much
to do with famine. It's better to loan animals
than to sell them. What made me vulnerable
was the exchange rate in publishing, the
animal to cereal ratio, and the price of blood.

At the end, after 10 years of use,
a government stooge burned our home,
and we abandoned the woody fallow
along Mud Creek, but the disturbances
involving water, light, and competition
have not declined, and to this day
I have not seen a field that was flat,
with a flat water table. I was hurt
by competition in an unproductive area.
I still sometimes see bushy pastures,
and the variants, plots and subplots
including replicates within a line, but
my love was clipped at ground level
and my interactions were lost that day.

Sometimes names are not better than
nothing, and it's more efficient to copy.
Sometimes advantages break down,
the crowd begins to conform and
no longer reflects the particular.
Today I came to think of imagination
as speculation, as a cascade of shells
that flows from words to meaning,
as if at first we were only playing
because we didn't really mean it
and weren't actively taking part.
But now we write our memos from
a place where disposition diverges
and it seems it is the meaning of
love's glance that loads the pause
and we think to play a more active role.
Now I know love plays well in Houston
too, and even if the gist of the passage
isn't familiar, whenever I remember
there's a little play in the moving parts,
I'm reminded the scoop about
guesswork is that everyone hopes for
a moving part in the immanent by and by.

Here follows the pathway
of form, a story of ritualized
sex, starvation and synergy,
a simple model with a linear
plot about the conditions of
dominance in which the models
are derivative recombinations
and have limitations. When
it comes to the distribution
of mutants, it seems the plot
is either skewed or close
to the curve, and the results
are not similar. Too often the
expression of one prevents
the expression of the other.
The concentration of writers
of orderly passages at the
na na national level increases
by day, but thankfully decreases
at night when the wild types
can plot and move closer.

Similar is within walking distance,
and different is a world apart.
I don't drive machinery, and I live
outside the hierarchy. Northern
rurals are imposed wherever
a fixed order of words coalesce
into place. See here, I'm nearby,
near to fear in the gaps between
the network where systems of lines
and people are all around me.
Every day the routines go on, a
desire to live at the edge of a field
because they say the countryside is
more peaceful, and there aren't as
many people in the mountains.
But I didn't like the country and
lived in a village that wasn't friendly.

Through the grey wood, along the banks,
then by the fields and cars, thomas moore
walked up the taylor river, up to martin's flats.
Lewis clarke had a cabin past scott hill.
Thomas was a petty case from newman bush
and he loved the griffin burns. Duncan olson,
an armstrong carpenter, lives there now,
on the snyder greene where the sweet
loves curry power. Belford notes the many
long brooks of the taylor, a brown river.
but stone duns were on the water. Wilder
english rivers rush for weeks but the story
is stark: little stanley welch dug graves
for miles behind the richmond meadows.

I used to want to mow the grass, and then
I tried to have it grazed. Next I wanted
a transect in the direction of away from
the grassland people because white men
want to let the light in. Needles and litter
accumulate wherever I've lived. I was sick
of the insistence toward light and openness,
and the loss of variance, and I missed
the beneficial marginal effects of poetry.
I wanted to talk about the relationship
between vascular language and the succession
to woodland thinking because remote areas
are no longer profitable and succession is
initiated when grasslands are abandoned.
The land I farmed was cold and rainy—
before I came along, it was deforested
and burned, but now it is not used anymore.

I live north of the Quesnel Blackwater
juncture, where the limited resolution
of America's moving faults gives way
to frequent bad news. Languages grind
against one another beneath the surface
of this shallow gouging. In these post-
Nechako times, I write complex histories
of vertical motion along America's
unimportant contours. It's true
Winnipegosis is located in basement
faults too, but in the Prince George fault
zone, it's also true local deformations
change from place to place. And there
are other faults with the local. The borehole
network is now loaded with slipping mistakes
in the sediments far below the surface.

But not all geopoems within the rift
are available for interpretation.
Stations log on the arriving waves,
spread along the lines, and bounce
out of the gate—first on one side, and
then the other. Sinuous and extensive,
faults flatten out below the surface.
Northern faults run through the area.
There are many paths of leakage
at the same time, and several faults
on line two, but rock mechanics penetrate
through the surface of shallow
interpretations and lies to the east.

Usually passive,
he signalled her impatience,
suggesting the Fraser fault zone is imaged—
citing a paper (Kroetsch, 1964),
which by and large dissolved meaning
west of the prairie evaporite.
More to the northwest,
I came to a particular oral evidence,
although limited to a few examples
and far away.
There are several faults on line eight,
and some between the lines
but they appear to play a role.

I'm not dry, but variable in my fertility.
Rocks are reds and stars are blue, melts
drain and collect, and they break and
deform and creep. The standard theory
of constraint means Lagrange multipliers
are normally phased as optimizers but
I'm earth's figure, my waves and tides
filtered out, and subject to constraint.
My lover ranges the height of the sea,
and my relief features match the floor.
It's a split-level scheme that keeps me
pristine so I can write feature lines, third
and fourth order derivatives about an
internal solitary wave of depression.
But when amplitude ridges oppose causes,
constraint is represented as a black dot.
When our plates cool, and we delaminate
and sink, our together limit moves along
the constraint line, and the minimum occurs
when the vectors point in opposite
directions, which is not what we want.

And then it turned cold again
and my thoughts turned to the north,
to landscapes of imaginary places and
all the video over time, to the ambient
metaphors of an edited landscape.
For some reason I migrated across forms,
turned the house upside down,
and switched to a different setting.
The flow spilled through the pasture
and I strayed from my place. Now
I'm starting a small periodical on-
line, and shooting the voice in May,
taking long takes and repetitive loops—
snippets of the moving image,
where the bank is undercut, and
eventually the tree falls into the river.

The time to hear animals is before a rain,
before the winds that bring it in, when
the wire is dumb, the cottonwoods grumble
and the spruce whistles its gliding pitch.
When the morning sky is clear and the air
is filled with sounds travelling far and wide,
periodic waves of sound spread out over
the land and do not rise above it, but roll out
over the hills and hollows. Fall fast, famous
tongue, make a full noise made of iron.
Often the Blackwater is nearly silent and
all things rock to sleep in the pervasive lull.
The wave front of my boat travelling through it
slips fastest when the sun is first on the water,
and I am carried along by the weather
as I surf the gathering swells and sinks.

A new subtype of a familiar,
I have a low competitive ability
and live on rocky shores while
my ex occurs on a brushy hillside
of Nass valley tuff. I'd like to be
an abandoned pasture with
completely degraded soils.
(Also see the weed species
in the ditches of the Hart.)
I write over the growing season
until shaded out by narrow endism.
My root-to-shoot ratio along the non-
managed roads of the Skeena and
in my neighbours' abandoned pastures
and glade-like areas where the river falls
is where the secondary succession I love
progresses past old fields and blue licks.

In this there will be nothing new
to turn from. The old hat sketched
earlier registers yesterday's remains,
and although it is my disposition
to expose faults with the werod
of the folkes, even those we know
nothing of signify disbelief. I'm
not a Saxon writer who pleases,
but full of fight, and a more popular
form, a miscreant, a hearer given
to drink, and what came in my way
was made up of substances grown
together into the currency of the
toft, passed from hand to hand
as borrowed words, which was
the more remarkable when we know
Anglo-Saxon is less in use where
the use of embellishment is avoided
and a derivative vernacular is spoken.

Once I was dependent on my tools
but now I'm not so sure. It seems
the acceptance of risk is a science,
but with pathogenic language,
examples of risk are infected with
subprime mutants, and the theories
of poetry have never been unified.
Poetry can make something more
dangerous than its parts, and this
is why the consequence of reading
a poem is unpredictable. The body
is weather, the mind is a wetland,
instincts come and go, responses
evolve and signals mix, but making
cheese goes back to the acceptance
of uncertainties. Don't stand alone.
Influence is never remote, and flows
almost everywhere, including the
strands of the flu. The manipulated
body of the pig is planned in secrecy
and leads to improbability, but it's
a good idea to burn the GE crops.

Ostracism is a piece of the western machine,
of which unity and consensus is the expectation,
but money doesn't determine real influence
because symbiosis is the path to survival.
Bacteria solve problems, and biology is
a mechanical theory about men.
Engineering doesn't always work out with pigs
despite the appearance of the barn
but the fixed linear sequence of
bacon-flavoured repetitive copies
are the passive carriers of instructions,
and it helps to emigrate.

The effect of one condition on another
is a vernacular, an assurance,
a familiar ambience in the reeky air.
Birds are portents, influences that play upon me,
and I'm inclined to answer yes
when solid shoals of whitefish are feeding fast
and the crows are going home to roost.
Cold rains chill the surface of the lake,
and the gulls sit in rows, looking for a wind.

Insects emigrate
and brain size is irrelevant.
Insects deserve better treatment.
E is for entry,
and an entry is a claim for land.
Field notes are kept in field books,
and holes are full of memories.
It's my job to fill holes.
I think of the reflex of the Sundew
when I think of things
like the love I tried to get.
Plants eat light.
They just sit around.
But with us,
the mind is near the mouth.
Sometimes researchers lack intelligence
and can't find the way back,
like bees.

One never knows what's about to happen
in relationships between things, but
I'm attracted to my skin bag outer clothing.
There's a sensual feeling when I put it on.
The strap is attached by an umbilical cord.
The double skin is a little cold at first,
and when I look at myself in the mirror,
and see my numbered bag with text,
logos and images transferred in,
I have a silhouette I've never seen before.

Depleted and wrecked,
I was fishing for gaga
and the make-believe
when you happened onto me,
a sap who couldn't tell
a conceit from an illusion.
I guess it's the law of averages
some call the breaks
but you ran a risk
and gave me a chance
when I had nothing to say.
Harlequin, the byword for reason
might be affinity,
but the off-chance odds of luck are
obscure and nearby no more,
and memories of you blow over
since I've been assigned
a better place
where I'm going halvers
with my good fortune.

I wear a black hat.
I have a cold. I'm a creature
of habit, even of bad ones.
Among other things I'm a jackal,
a joker, a second-nature virus,
the appearance and go-between clue,
the figure of seen. I have an eye
for disposition and a trust of makeup.
I'm Amber, Amber forever.
I'm a normal teenage girl from Hixon.
I could be property and be forever
yours, remembered forever after.
I could go to makeup school, take
makeup education, go to makeup
college, fall in love and make up forever.
I could write forever fantasies
that start where the others stop,
publish in a forever cemetery, be
in a library of lives, shelved next
to bullets forever. I have
active dirty tendencies.
Narrow mind, narrow soul.

One can only understand
what happens. Now and again
I pick up and piece together
the lines and measures of literal holdings
such as the canon, and I think of
the forms texts assume about slavery,
the jealous and clever code of laws
that suit the national narrative.
Many authors live up to the promise
and social context of the slave narrative,
circulating specific cultural memories
that work very hard, making again and again
the literary form of the subject,
the plodding beasts of burden, the playthings,
the anecdotal versions, the slave poems
so loved by the white readers of the north.

The canon's bad news.
The ties of blood
between having land and power
isn't an ambiguous nostalgia,
but now that I have fallen in with
those who favour a shuffle,
it's time to split the difference
and smooth it over.
I'm wanting to neutralize
the textual forces of the manager's mob,
and write a new subject because
I'm not property, but the sure sign
of territory and occupancy.

Reading is the high water mark of
influence, the borderline of master-slave
relations between type and readership,
the line between fluency and form.
Before I disrupted the narrative purity
of the republic, back when persuasion
and phylums began to pick up speed,
before the scenery of revisionism,
before the flood, when I couldn't buy
my way out of yesterday's story,
before the fall, before the imagined
reformation, before the war, before
the sleight of hand, before the price
of cotton, the meaning in the story
was the slave who rose to murder
the definition of the master, publishing
was brokered by bias and blood.

All but broke, I lived an indigent's life,
forcy, down to earth, never far from
lingual phonemics, but I remember
the charity and coherence of living
in the lull, in the comfort of silence,
when, after day, was alone in my
12 by 14 winter wall tent, where
not in a cottage, but a covering,
I'd compose my disposition and
affinity for tomorrow. I rested
on a planed lumber bed, beside
an airtight stove, not the big one,
but the next down, set inside a
rigid frame of drawknifed Balsam
poles wired at the crotch, floor
stapled to a deck I ripped. And
when the day was over, after
drying off and warming up, I'd
move outside to listen in the open
air, in the dark. A call so low
you'd miss it or think there was
nothing to it, and then, an answer.

Absent from the Yucatán Peninsula,
but heard as far north as New York
in hills and ravines, in the old forest
fragments, in the roots of blow-down
trees near muddy toxic streams and
fallen leaves, singing a complex jumble
of short rapidly uttered phrases,
large bodied, with long heavy feet,
ground dweller, primarily picks at
the pain of others, dreams in a cup
made of moss, departs after pairing.

Only a few I know of come to church,
and I am not approved of, but live
by what name and by what code
with my degenerate, retreating
faith. And by this means, consider
the fantastic imagination of
Christians, how they shout
their gospels that leave no doubt.
And the lie is presented to children
in terms of image and story
as something of more authority
than a reflection that cancels the
effects of experience, the agents
of transmission being adults and
the dark matter of the lyric.

Generally speaking, the personal
is materialistic and not a pronoun,
but a convenient antecedent
on autopilot, a backseat driver
who thinks the cowherd calls
the shots. Many critics seem to be
disembodied drovers teaching
image recognition. I was lounging
in a poetry arcade when someone
hacked into my face and instantly
I knew it was my fairy godmother
editor when I heard her say open
your eyes, oni. The authorities will
never forget the face of poetry, so
in that sense, poems look like the
poets who make them. And we can
also forget about temptation, even
if we know it's bound to happen.

Geared to the dirty work and
burdened with the grind of business,
I agreed to a boost for sweetening
the conceptual, copied a billet,
and brought it down onto the bolt
with everything I had. My father-in-law,
who remains unforgettable, and was
a ruling figure, was a man of
degenerative change, but also
of consequence and charm, always
looked out-of-place on the main
drag, but not on a corduroy road.
He was the first born who was John,
the oldest, the second cousin,
an ancestor to a bear, a vagrant
son derived from the unknown
mother who, in the story, disappeared.

I'm pleased Devil's Lake is rising,
flooding pasturelands, roads and
homes. This lake rose and fell
before the field studies and now
it's something about wood and bone
and the frequency of flooding in
the channels. Through every outlet
that is exposed long enough for soil
to develop, longtime readers and
most residents of North Dakota
submitted samples from the horizons
to the Water Board. There's sedimentation
at the openings, standing water now
and a chain of marshy lowlands
before a well defined, narrow exit.

I bit into a persimmon and the weather
on the other side of town seemed murky
and sour, not because it was still and
without explanation, but a skip. It's
just what happens. After all, nothing
is restricted to straight lines, and
the reflective surface of the page is
sometimes cool and cold, or warm and hot.
And there, by the edge of a weary pond,
smelled the ba and bit and breath of life,
for the earth does breathe, and flicked
a match and smoked in the breathing place
where phenomena are not perceptions,
but drag one weary foot after another.
And in the fetid air, inhaled and exhaled,
and stayed a while, for something like
a happy hour in the brush, for a puff
of air and a puff of smoke and a rest
in the steam and stench of suggestion.

The uniformly creamy Eastern Racer
spends the day basking or gliding
over ground in search of poems.
Generally absent from forested hillsides,
these residents of the open grassland
and pastures are able to crawl faster
than you or I can walk. Racers milk cows
and crawl back and forth over horse-hair
ropes, and their tongues tickle.
Wear protective clothing, and never
go to readings alone. Stay on paths,
watch where you go, and never
stick your hands inside their pants.

In a small body of slowly moving water,
in the shadow of a Balsam sweeper,
laying still in the common supply of
the warmer waters of the lake, five
pairs each a metre long, they'd been
together all their lives, surfing yesterday
up the river in a pod. I knew because
I saw them enter, saw the arrangement,
the awareness, the commodities they
paid for with their lives, and I knew
the price was fixed. But I headed out
because the water was slowing, and
pans were forming in the bay. And then
in May I returned, my shadow on the river
once again. There they were in the rising
water, and I knew they remembered me
because there was something conscious
in that eye-to-eye flicker in the instant
before the waters turned and I carried on.

When speaking of the weather
we think of perceptions
and not of readings.
The weather changes quickly.
Climate is what we expect but
the weather is what we get.
The weather argues with the colour
but the application is
the pneumatic movement of the line.
The weather doesn't repeat itself.
I cover the weather
and then we get our information
from the network and after that
we talk about the weather,
the shade and shadow of continuity.
Climate wears away at code
and code is the mood
of the intension of nature.
The weather wore me ragged
but I rode it out, and came around the back,
but when I look at those gloomy skies
I'm ready to sell at whatever price.

To the extent that I am able,
my poems are flexible accumulations
having to do with the special fit of desire
to laws. The long past of my family
has collapsed and I now live
in a continuous present.
I intervene in the local with poetry.
To the extent that I can,
I know myself and what I have done
and I aspire to something more
than self-indulgence
or even self-sufficiency.
If I could, I would like to restore
the subject of narrative
to other composite descriptions
limned in my disillusionment
with the land, the subject
placed into the centre of
the experience of the poem,
my investment in the subject,
when the narrative shifts, postponed.

It's a long way to the suburbs
and the mothers in my bloodstream,
who are inclined to forget
even their own basic propositions
and blood-loving influences
are in spontaneous decline.
Ditto the absent-minded.
The picture changes when
epidemics too small to be seen
combine with the repetitious.
Commonly called the disease
that is never absent,
complications come along
and spread very fast after intimacy.
Carriers break down when
we linger and are sloppy.
Parts of the poem drift, and
language so old it seems new
lives peacefully in the mouth where
words mutate into slaves.
Everyone recovers and
we custom the common denominator
with non-stick coatings
for room and board in our throats.

I am a poet and not ashamed,
not afraid of being believed,
not afraid of breaking up my family,
not entangled in or derived from flaws.
My poems are not presented in desire
or disguise, and I'm not afraid of rejection,
The land I lived in was not unsafe,
and I lived, not according to importance,
but where systems overlapped and
returning uncles were tolerated.
Nothing is wrong in this poem but
I'm inclined to speculate as to why
my memories of families I knew
on the ranches and farms did not
distinguish between silences
and fears too strong to break.

There's more chaos in a healthy
heart than a sick one. Men can
make a mess out of anything but
beauty is at the beginning of selection.
Meteorites can fall, chaos isn't scary,
and these coal cars, supported by
the inland biomass are moveable
consequences at evolution's edge.
Derailings happen more often now.
It takes generations to find out
who went into the trees, and who
ran in place, but this big brown
smoke's increasing scale seems
to be the result of intended trophic
consequences according to others.

Labrador forms Ungava Bay.
Off the coast, the shelf travels
east to the sea. Empty now,
the Grand Banks lie in the south,
where skinny tides bore across
the North American shallow plate.
Massive winds blow off the land,
the spring ice mixes, and some of
the fog banks along the coast.
Thousands of species originate
in the column off Witless Island
where the boundary comes ashore
at the tip of Avalon. Large numbers
winter in the open. There are stars
beneath the ice, worms below the
mud and fears the size of small
mountains. No longer sustainable,
all are named, some are indigenous,
and some migrate through.

If a word is made of a thousand images,
then whose words, what words? Is it
because, or is it the arc of narrative of
the image industry, or the fiction that
is on the film in the box that has a lens?
Is it a form that no longer makes sense?
A stream of worn-out representations,
the inclination of habits by necessity
left behind? This world is not the best
one, but time is still to come, and the past
is moving more quickly than the future.
The endless misery of the Canadian image
and the pretence of unity is familiar, but
there is something common that is not land,
or something seen, not animal or plant, not
a courtesy or field, not a pasture for cattle,
but more a book colonized with images,
and it is not what I had hoped for.

At the Sansixmor, the boreal
wester is bleak, but fresh, and
the fabulous north can hardly be
believed: a concoction made up
in the mind and not based in fact—
or an adopted fiction with
a large amount of fantasy in it.
This isn't about making something up,
or make-believe, or imagined, in play.
Oh, figmental, forged deception
based on the old stories, which
are probably not true, who
hatched you, and what are
your activities? What is your promise
and why are you so unreal?

Low class, and talked about many times,
I wandered down the hill in a husky body
resembling you and me, a sharecropper
left with food. I started out, not by playing
a part, but living a life of my own, the
exquisite experience of a fifty-fifty particular,
not as an individual, but by an incidental turn
of events, and the choicy brass tacks I wrote
over the decades, however defined, were parsed
through pens. Some was bannock and some was
bagels, but I don't have a fictional identity, or
another form of by you, or for you. Those who
bought my books were able to imagine me,
and being neighbours, have not asked that
I abandon my own knowing, but most were men.
I write, not in the bonds of harmony, or of
collaboration, or of the cement of friendship,
and when I moved away, last I heard,
my readers buttered their bagels with mayo.

When I fell in with poetry, I found
something I could not account for,
something within, a jurisdictional
conflict like the separation between
language and biologists that lie, or
models and maps that gave me
the word, and let me in. Guessing
is one explanation, but I'm curious
re: struggles about how to see
when descriptions shift, and listeners
are not convinced enough to say
the unspecifiable has meaning.
No one's able to resist the uncertainties
of pigs and flies and birds. Suppose
you are a representative travelling
with a new crowd now, well, I'll
root for the dialogues, any risk and
crush of confluences, any inference
of ambiguity that lies in charming
accuracy away with flies swarming
downwind in the margins.

The nature I knew is disappearing.
Mostly it's used in construction.
The nature I knew doesn't come clean.
It disobeys and bootlegs the unallowed.
The game shifts when turbulence reverses.
As a matter of fact, the low down
on the unwritten is, facts are mostly
handed down, and since they are fond
of society, get together for adventure.
In this, description is not countryside,
but is made of the after-effects of everything
that is, and the motion sickness I get happens
when the distinction between previews
of not only the context but also the content
becomes the subject of expanded energy,
an architecture of not only assembly
but also disposal, the disposition of form
having to do with mining and milling.

I drew a stick-phone and held it to my ear but
the guy in the next seat said "hello" and passed it back
to me, saying "it's for you." Memory is a file of pythons
moving slow and spectacles are a seeming sham
when inconsistencies collide. Soon spreads out
in many directions and cross-currents are not flaws
or incoherence, but exception and refusal. Forgotten
between a low water outflow, and a never-ending,
evergreen lumen, I'm for crooked sentences, but not
the hypocrisy of the image. Time stretches thin when
you're late, and if there are no contradictions, then
everything is under control. Moving clocks run slow.
The past is what nothing can be sent back to. To do so
would rest the present on confusions just when
something big is coming. If you go to second thoughts,
you'll find a variety of old and new clothing. And
people light fires when they can't take it anymore.
I'd sooner bang my pots and pans and burn chairs
to generate content than stand in the mall with a poster.
If you talk into a stick, you won't need much memory.

Although intensional, but not interesting,
(and that is part of life), my first marriage
seemed too full of meaning for both
metaphor and substance and I had to
go somewhere else. Later on I noticed
the next thing after the buy and sell
moment of empathy was the discord,
times distance, that goes with divorce
after the deal. And when I think of the barter
that goes on when telling fish stories
and pious fiction, it seems to be a good
thing we miss a few typos. Green means
go but snow is white and isn't the same
sort of thing. It seems something I can do,
even while soaking in the softness of
the look of my silver-tongued sloka, is
draw conclusions, maybe even get some-
thing for something. Everybody knows
the whole story requires assumptions and
takes place by saying things. But what
it might be, I'm not always able to tell.

Swarms, composed of hundreds of events
stretching from the background states
to the river, are indigenous to the immediate,
and this fast groundwater flow still occurs
in the upper Muskabou, where a conductivity
corresponding to other transcurrent structures
and western faults is unlike the fault lines
now encircling the interior, crossing, and then
crossing-out the living veins, the love-wave
brought to the surface, the eroded low
water structure collapsing the clouds, and
now we hold those faults in our hands.

I give away words for a living.
Sometimes I'm the running title,
others the saw and scene, period.
I'm analect and battledore, and
I want to know, but I get into trouble
when I ask the wrong questions.
And Eve failed, and thinking of,
for example, the final warning,
the draft, the contents and copy
and cue, as well as the variants
and versions of the word, it is the leaf
and line and living mot that I bring
home to this book, something that is
more about injustice than in error, so
I hand down this workbook hint
and say, like me, leave words, and
allow these poems to bend and
cause to be, and come apart again.